My Little Book of
Ocean Life

by Camilla de la Bédoyère

Sandy Creek
NEW YORK

An Imprint of Sterling Publishing
387 Park Avenue South
New York, NY 10016

Text © 2014 by QEB Publishing, Inc.
Illustrations © 2014 by QEB Publishing, Inc.

This 2014 edition published by Sandy Creek.

ISBN 978-1-4351-5528 2

Manufactured in Guangdong, China
Lot #:
2 4 6 8 10 9 7 5 3 1
04/14

Contents

Coral Polyps

A **coral reef** is home to many **ocean** animals. The reef is built by animals called coral **polyps**.

∨ **There are many types of coral in a reef.**

« **A polyp grabs animals with its** tentacles **and pulls them into its mouth to eat them.**

Coral reefs grow in sunny places, where the water is warm and clean. Polyps have soft bodies but they build a stony skeleton around themselves.

⌃ **This type of coral is called a brain coral.**

Sea Anemone

Sea anemones are soft, squishy animals. They live on the seabed, in shallow water.

⌄ **The sea anemone's body is a long tube. At the top is a mouth that is surrounded by tentacles.**

« **Clownfish stay safe by hiding from** predators **inside an anemone. It does not sting them.**

The tentacles are covered in stings. When an animal swims through them, it is stung and then swallowed.

« Little boxer crabs wave sea anemones at their enemies to scare them!

7

Sea Urchin

Sea urchins are prickly animals. They have sharp spines that stop many animals from eating them.

⌄ The sea urchin's body is round and hard with long spines.

« This sea urchin is being attacked by some starfish.

The mouth of a sea urchin is on its bottom! Sea urchins move slowly along rocks, eating small animals and **algae**.

>> This little crab stops other animals from eating it by carrying a sea urchin.

Starfish

Most starfish have five arms. They use them to crawl along the seabed as they hunt for food.

Starfish are also called "sea stars." They push their stomachs out of their mouths to capture and eat shellfish.

⌄ **This starfish is growing new arms.**

<< A crown-of-thorns starfish.

>> These blue starfish are crawling over soft ocean animals called sponges.

If a starfish loses an arm, it can grow a new one.

Jellyfish

A jellyfish has long, stinging tentacles. Some jellyfish are tiny, but others can grow to be as big as a man.

⌄ **This jellyfish has trapped a fish in its tentacles.**

⌃ **A mauve stinger has stings on both its tentacles and in the little red spots on its body.**

Jellyfish use their stings to stun or kill fish. They cannot swim very well so they must travel where the ocean carries them.

⌃ **This deep sea medusa jellyfish lives in the deep ocean.**

Sea Slug

Sea slugs are snails that live in the ocean. They do not have shells to protect their soft body.

❧ **This beautiful sea slug is called a "blue dragon."**

Sea slugs have a clever way to stay safe. Their bright colors warn animals that they have deadly poison in their skin. Some sea slugs have stings, too.

>> As a sea slug crawls along the seabed, it eats small animals, such as sponges and coral polyps.

Shellfish

Shellfish live on seabeds all over the world. They usually live in shallow water and eat other animals.

« A giant clam is over three feet long.

⌄ A conch pokes its head out of its shell.

Shellfish are cousins of snails and octopuses. They have a shell and tentacles. They also have a rough tongue that is covered with tiny teeth.

⌄ A cone shell can fire a poison dart from a special tube. These shellfish eat fish and worms.

Octopus

Octopuses are some of the smartest animals in the ocean. They have a big brain and very good eyesight.

>> This is a Pacific giant octopus. It can grow up to more than 9 feet long.

An octopus has a round body, large eyes, and eight arms. It crawls along the seabed, but it is also a good swimmer.

⌃ Octopuses grab fish with the suckers on their arms.

Peacock Mantis Shrimp

Peacock mantis shrimps are stunning animals. They are covered in beautiful colors.

≪ **This shrimp is hiding in her** burrow **where she looks after her little red eggs.**

Peacock mantis shrimps are cousins to crabs and lobsters. They live in warm, shallow water and hunt other animals.

Peacock mantis shrimps attack using their powerful front legs, which are strong enough to break glass!

« Most shrimps are smaller than a little finger, but peacock mantis shrimps can grow up to 8 inches long.

21

Crab

Crabs live under the ocean, but they spend time on the seashore, too. These ocean animals have a strong, shell-like skin.

⌃ **A fiddler crab's eyes are on long stalks.**

Crabs have five pairs of legs and can run fast across a sandy beach. At the front of the crab's body are claws that can be used to catch other animals.

⌄ **This is a Sally Lightfoot crab.**

» **Japanese spider crabs live in the deep ocean.**

Lobster

Lobsters can grow over three feet long. Like crabs, they have a tough outer skin and lots of legs.

Lobsters live underwater and are good swimmers. They use their claws to grab and crack open shellfish before eating their soft insides.

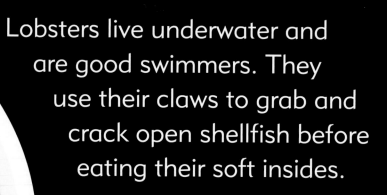

« **Spiny lobsters** migrate **to cold, deep water.**

⌄ Squat lobsters have crab-like bodies.

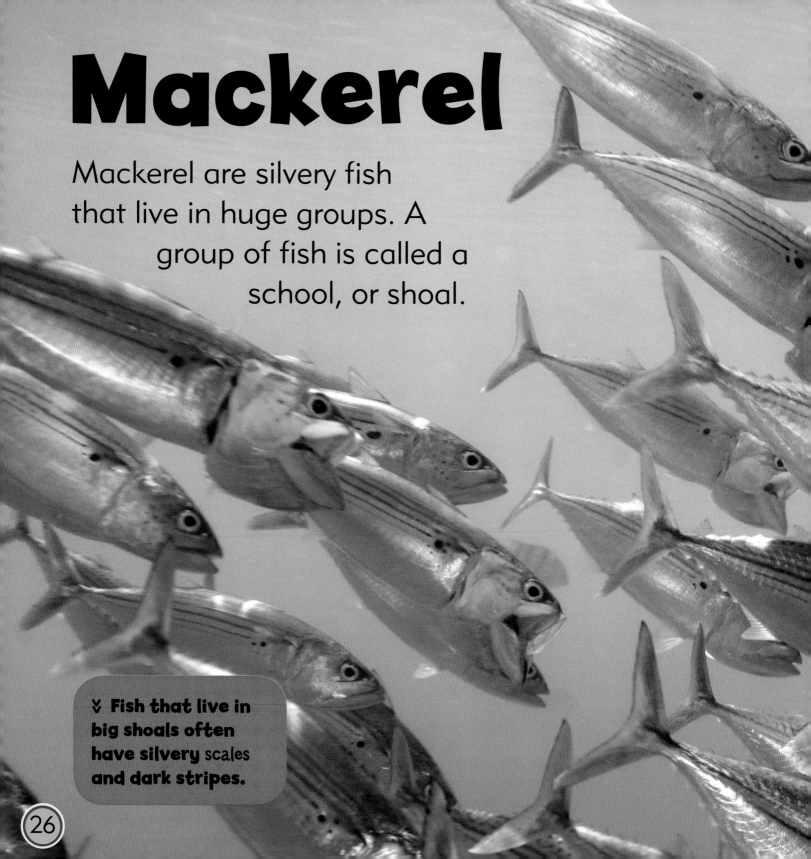

Mackerel

Mackerel are silvery fish that live in huge groups. A group of fish is called a school, or shoal.

⌄ **Fish that live in big shoals often have silvery** scales **and dark stripes.**

⌃ **This shark is hunting a shoal of fish.**

Mackerel are fast swimmers that twist and turn to avoid other animals. Seabirds, whales, sharks, and other bony fish all hunt mackerel.

Coral Fish

Coral fish live around coral reefs, where there is plenty of food to eat and many places to hide.

⌄ **Lionfish have a big mouth and sharp spines.**

« **Triggerfish nibble at animals and plants on the seabed.**

Fish have **fins** and scales. Most coral fish have bold colors or patterns.

⌄ **Wrasse fish eat tiny pieces of food inside the mouth of a sweetlips fish.**

Seahorse

Seahorses are unusual little fish. They are so weak they can hardly swim.

>> Seahorses wrap their tails around seaweed **so they are not swept away.**

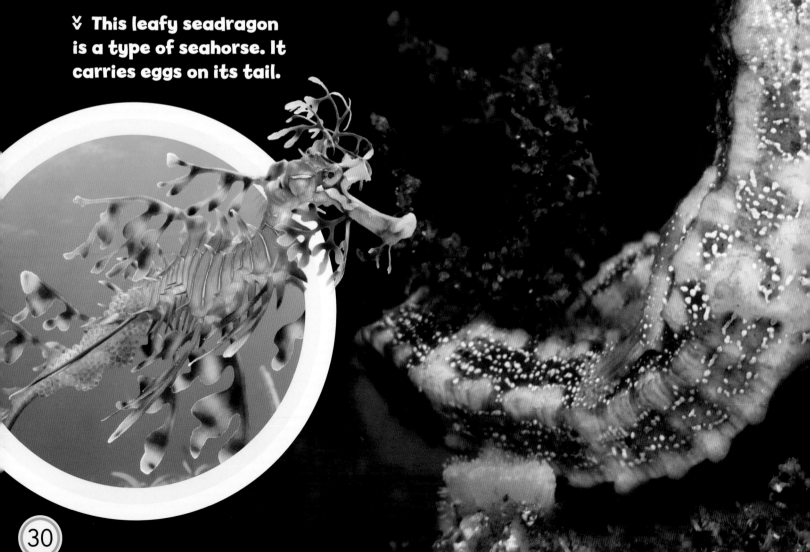

⌄ This leafy seadragon is a type of seahorse. It carries eggs on its tail.

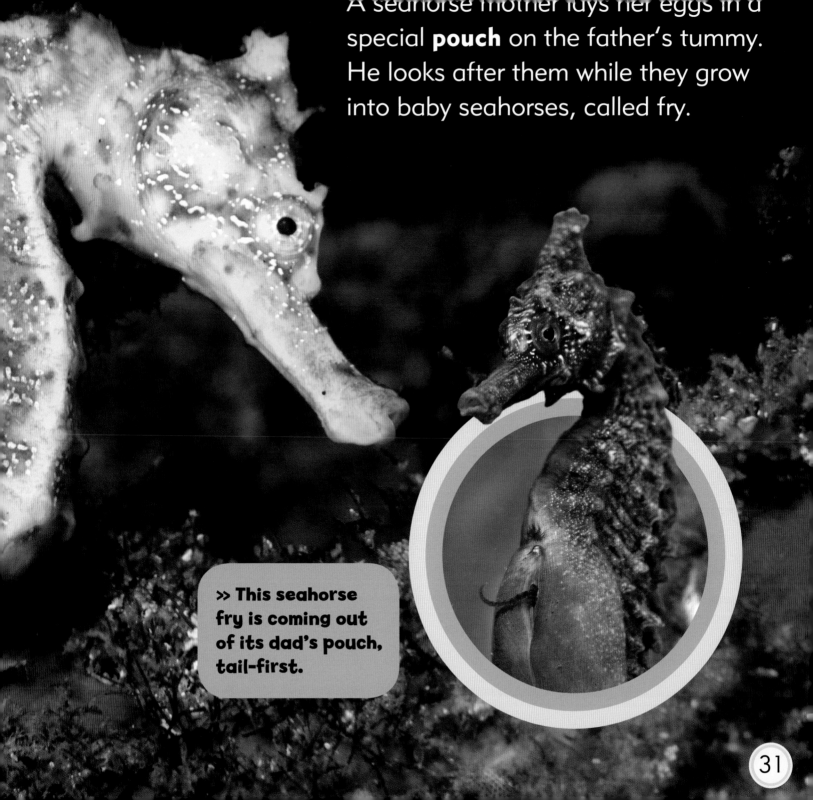

A seahorse mother lays her eggs in a special **pouch** on the father's tummy. He looks after them while they grow into baby seahorses, called fry.

>> This seahorse fry is coming out of its dad's pouch, tail-first.

Ray

Rays are flat fish that can grow to an enormous size. Some manta rays are the same size as a car!

⌄ **This ray has blue spots and stripes, and a sharp spine at the base of its tail.**

« **A manta ray can grow up to 22 feet wide. It swims by flapping its big fins.**

Rays have a long tail and wing-like fins. Their **gills** are on the underside of their body. Rays are good swimmers, but often rest on the seabed.

⌃ The pattern on a torpedo ray's skin helps it to hide on the seabed.

Shark

Sharks are fierce, powerful fish that hunt other ocean animals.

> ∨ **The great white shark has rows of sharp teeth in its mouth.**

> ≪ **Great white sharks can leap out of the water.**

>> **This shark
is called a
hammerhead shark.**

There are about
500 types of shark.
Most sharks use their
amazing sense of smell
to find animals to eat.

35

Marine Iguana

Most lizards live on land, but these big lizards dive into the ocean, too.

>> Marine iguanas are large lizards. They can grow up to three feet long.

<< Marine iguanas can hold their breath underwater for up to one hour.

Marine iguanas dive underwater so they can nibble on seaweeds. When they are not eating, marine iguanas sunbathe on rocks.

Sea Snake

Most snakes slither on the ground, but sea snakes are super swimmers.

Banded sea kraits have a paddle-shaped tail that helps them swim. They hunt fish, especially eels.

⌃ **This is a yellow-lipped sea krait.**

« This sea snake has slithered on to the land to lay its eggs.

» Sea kraits have **sharp** fangs **and a deadly bite.**

Turtle

Turtles go on amazing journeys across the ocean. They travel far to find food, and to lay their eggs.

⌄ **After hatching from their eggs, baby turtles walk to the ocean.**

⌃ **Loggerhead turtles are large** reptiles **that grow up to three feet long.**

Loggerhead turtles have a large head and strong jaws. They live in the sea, but they breathe air.

⌄ Turtles can crush shellfish, crabs, and lobsters in their beak-like mouth.

41

Saltwater Crocodile

Saltwater crocodiles are the largest crocodiles in the world. They are sometimes called "salties."

>> A crocodile's snout is long and thin. It contains about 66 sharp teeth.

>> Crocodiles breathe air. This crocodile will soon swim to the surface to breathe.

Salties can reach to about 22 feet long. They live near the seashore, **swamps**, or where rivers meet the sea.

Crocodiles hunt at night and eat birds and fish.

>> Young crocodiles push their tails into the water to leap up into the air.

Penguin

Penguins are ocean birds and great swimmers. They have black and white feathers.

>> Macaroni penguins have a crest **of golden feathers.**

<< **Baby penguins are small and very fluffy.**

⌃ **Penguins swim far
and deep to find food.**

Macaroni penguins live near
the **South Pole**, where the water
is very cold. Like all penguins,
they hunt for fish in the ocean
and lay their eggs on land.

Albatross

Albatrosses are huge ocean birds. They spend most of their lives soaring above the ocean.

« Albatross parents build a nest on land, and look after their chick **together.**

⌃ An albatross's wingspan can measure more than 9 feet.

Albatrosses are some of the largest flying birds in the world. They dive into the water to catch fish with their long **beaks**.

>> **It can take years for an albatross to find its perfect mate.**

Sea Otter

Sea otters have thick fur to keep them warm in cold water. They spend most of the time in the ocean.

>> Sea otters wrap themselves in seaweed so they do not float away.

⌄ Sea otters sometimes float in a group, called a raft, and even hold hands!

Most otters live in rivers, but sea otters live in the Pacific Ocean. They even give birth in the water and look after their cubs there.

⌄ **Sea otters eat shellfish. They bash the shells with rocks to reach the soft animals inside.**

49

Seal

Seals are strong swimmers. They use their flipper and tail to speed through the ocean as they hunt for fish.

>> A seal's thick fur keeps it warm, even in icy water.

⌄ A seal uses its flippers to change direction.

These mammals have a
thick layer of fat to keep
them warm. Young seals
are called pups and
they feed on their
mother's milk.

Walrus

Walruses are large, heavy animals that live in the cold **Arctic Ocean**.

>> A walrus's tusks are long teeth that can grow up to three feet long!

Walruses have wrinkly, pinkish brown skin; tusks; and flippers. They use their sensitive whiskers to find shellfish on the seabed.

⌃ **Walruses gather in** colonies **to rest on land.**

≫ **Walruses use their tusks to heave themselves up onto slippery ice.**

Dolphin

Dolphins are small whales with long snouts that are called beaks. They are smart, friendly animals.

>> Dolphins have long, slender bodies that are the perfect shape for swimming fast in the world's oceans.

<< Dolphins like to leap through the air. This is called "porpoising."

54

Dolphins dive deep to find fish and **squid** to eat. They live in family groups called pods. There may be hundreds of dolphins in one pod.

>> Dolphins swim to the ocean's surface when they need to breathe.

Sperm Whale

Sperm whales are the world's largest hunters. They eat octopuses, fish, and squid.

>> **Although sperm whales breathe air, they can stay underwater for up to two hours at a time.**

A sperm whale has the biggest brain of any animal that has ever lived. It dives into deep, cold water to find food.

⌄ **Sperm whales are about 50 feet long. They can weigh as much as 10 elephants!**

57

Blue Whale

This is the largest animal that has ever lived on Earth. A blue whale's tongue is the size of an elephant!

⌄ **A baby blue whale is called a calf and it feeds on its mother's milk.**

Blue whales may be huge, but they eat tiny ocean animals called **krill**. They open their mouths to suck in water. Then they gulp down all the krill in that mouthful of water.

⌄ Blue whales live near the surface of the ocean.

⌃ Whales breathe using a blowhole. When a blue whale breathes out, the spray can shoot 30 feet into the air!

Glossary

algae Plants that do not grow roots or flowers. Most algae live in the ocean.

Arctic Ocean The cold ocean at the North Pole.

beak The long, slender mouth of a bird or a dolphin.

burrow A hole or tunnel that is an animal's home.

chick A young bird.

colonies Groups of animals of one type that all live together.

coral reef Stony places that have been built by polyps and make a good home for many other animals.

crest Colorful feathers on a bird's head.

fangs Sharp teeth.

fins Parts of an animal's body that are used for swimming.

gills The parts of an animal's body that are used for breathing underwater. Fish use gills to breathe.

krill Small, shrimp-like animals.

migrate To go on a long journey, usually to find food or a mate.

ocean A huge area of water. There are five oceans in the world: Pacific, Atlantic, Indian, Southern, and Arctic.

predators Animals that hunt and eat other animals.

polyps Small, soft-bodied animals with tentacles.

pouch A pocket-like place on an animal's body.

reptiles Animals with scaly skin. Most reptiles lay eggs.

scales The stiff, small "plates" that cover a fish's body.

seaweed Plants that grow in the ocean.

snout The nose and mouth of an animal.

South Pole The place at the bottom of the world.

squid Animals with a soft body and tentacles. Squid are similar to octopuses.

swamps Land by the ocean that is always wet. Some ocean animals live in swamps.

tentacles Long, bendy parts of an animal's body that can move to touch, hold, or sense things.

Index

Picture Credits

Alamy
7 bl RGB Ventures LLC dba SuperStock, 33 cr Robert Harding World Imagery, 45 tr National Geographic Image Collection.

Ardea
49 br Tom and Pat Leeson.

F1 Online
64 br.

FLPA
1 tl Sebastian Kennerknecht/Minden Pictures, 1 bl Thomas Marent/Minden Pictures, 1 cr Reinhard Dirscherl, 3 r Reinhard Dirscherl, 4–5 Reinhard Dirscherl, 4 bl Colin Marshall, 5 tr Pete Oxford/Minden Pictures, 6 bl Norbert Wu/ Minden Pictures, 8–9 Fred Bavendam/Minden Pictures, 8 bl Norbert Wu/Minden Pictures, 10–11 Colin Marshall, 10 bl Fred Bavendam/Minden Pictures, 11 tc Norbert Probst/Imagebroker, 12–13 Reinhard Dirscherl, 14–15 Michael Moxter/Imagebroker, 18–19 Brandon Cole/Biosphoto, 19 tr Jeffrey Rotman/Biosphoto, 20–21 J.W.Alker/ Imagebroker, 22–23 Malcolm Schuyl, 22 tc Thomas Marent/Minden Pictures, 24–25 ImageBroker/Imagebroker, 26–27 Imagebroker, 27 tr Mike Parry/Minden Pictures, 28–29 Pierre Lobel/Biosphoto, 28 bc Reinhard Dirscherl, 29 cr Imagebroker, 30–31 Norbert Probst/Imagebroker, 32–33 Reinhard Dirscherl, 34 Gerard Lacz, 35 Brandon Cole/ Biosphoto, 36–37 OceanPhoto, 36 cl Olivier Born/Biosphoto, 38–39 Colin Marshall, 38/39 tc Nicolas–Alain Peti/ Biosphoto, 39 br ImageBroker/Imagebroker, 40–41 Imagebroker, 40 bl Konrad Wothe/Minden Pictures, 42–43 Mike Parry, 43 tl Cyril Ruoso/Minden Pictures, 43 br Sylvain Cordier/Biosphoto, 44–45 Bill Coster, 44 cl Suzi Eszterhas/Minden Pictures, 46–47 Ingo Schultz/Imagebroker, 47 cr Tui De Roy/Minden Pictures, 48–49 Donald M. Jones/Minden Pictures, 49 tl Suzi Eszterhas/Minden Pictures, 50–51 Paul van Hoof/Minden Pictures, 50 cl Norbert Probst/Imagebroker, 53 tl Michio Hoshino/Minden Pictures, 53 br Bill Coster, 54–55 Flip Nicklin/Minden Pictures, 54 bl Hiroya Minakuchi/Minden Pictures, 55 cr Flip Nicklin/Minden Pictures, 56–57 Reinhard Dirscherl, 57 bc Norbert Wu/Minden Pictures, 58–59 Flip Nicklin/Minden Pictures, 60–61 Sylvain Cordier/Biosphoto, 62 cr Reinhard Dirscherl.

Nature Picture Library
2 l Wild Wonders of Europe/Zankl, 6–7 Sue Daly, 9 tr Jurgen Freund, 12 bl Sue Daly, 13 tr David Shale, 15 cr Jurgen Freund, 16–17 Franco Banfi, 16 cl Jurgen Freund, 17 br Jeff Rotman, 18 b Alex Mustard, 20 bl Brandon Cole, 23 br Doug Perrine, 24 bl Doug Perrine, 30 bl Alex Mustard, 31 cr Alex Mustard, 32 cr Franco Banfi, 34–35 David Fleetham, 41 br Doug Perrine, 46 bl Andy Rouse, 52–53 Danny Green, 58 bl Doc White, 59 tr Mark Carwardine, 63 br Andy Rouse.

Shutterstock
fc DJ Mattaar, bc Vudhikrai, SnBence, BMJ, Achimdiver, saiva, Jette Vis